OBOE   Book 3

ACCENT ON ACHIEVEMENT

John O'Reilly
and
Mark Williams

The "Keys" to Success: Progressive Technical & Rhythmic Studies in all 12 Major and 12 Minor Keys

Dear Band Student:

Congratulations on completing the first two books of
ACCENT ON ACHIEVEMENT. Book 3 will help you to develop
the musical and technical skills necessary for a lifetime of great
music-making. Your "Keys" to success include scales,
exercises and fun tunes in all 12 major and 12 minor keys.
You'll learn new rhythms and meters, and also improve your
tone and intonation while playing a rich variety of chorales.
With diligent practice, there's no end to what you can accomplish!
We wish you the best in your quest for musical excellence.

John O'Reilly   *Mark Williams*

John O'Reilly   Mark Williams

Instrument photos (cover and page 1) are courtesy of Yamaha Corporation of America.

Copyright © MCMXCIX Alfred Publishing Co., Inc.
All rights reserved. Printed in USA.

ACCENT ON CONCERT B♭ MAJOR

CHORALE: CHILDREN'S PRAYER from "HANSEL AND GRETEL"

Engelbert Humperdinck
(1854–1921)

B♭ MAJOR SCALE (CONCERT B♭)

INTERVAL WORKOUT

SCALE STUDY

CHROMATIC SCALE

ACCENT ON RHYTHM: $\frac{9}{8}$ Time

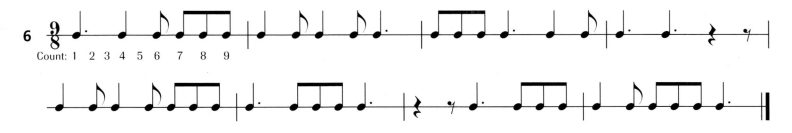

MORNING HAS BROKEN

Irish Folk Song

ACCENT ON RHYTHM: $\frac{12}{8}$ Time

ANDANTE CANTABILE from "SYMPHONY NO. 5"

Peter I. Tchaikovsky
(1840–1893)

ACCENT ON CONCERT G MINOR

CHORALE: BASED ON A THEME BY NEUMARK

Johann Sebastian Bach
(1685–1750)

ACCENT ON RHYTHM: $\frac{3}{2}$ Time

RONDO

Henry Purcell
(1659–1695)

THE WILD HORSEMAN

Robert Schumann
(1810–1856)

ACCENT ON CONCERT E♭ MAJOR

CHORALE: BE THOU MY VISION

Moderato

Traditional Irish Melody

E♭ MAJOR SCALE (CONCERT E♭)

INTERVAL WORKOUT

SCALE STUDY

CHROMATIC SCALE

ACCENT ON RHYTHM: ♪♩

THE KEEL ROW

Allegretto

English/Scottish Folk Song

ACCENT ON RHYTHM: ♫♩♩ and ♫♫♩♫

PETITE OISEAU

Moderato

Traditional

ACCENT ON CONCERT C MINOR

CHORALE: PRELUDE IN C MINOR

Frèdèric Chopin
(1810–1849)

C MELODIC MINOR SCALE (CONCERT C)

*See Fingering Chart on page 38.

INTERVAL WORKOUT

*See Fingering Chart on page 38.

SCALE STUDY

C HARMONIC MINOR SCALE (CONCERT C)

ACCENT ON RHYTHM: ♩♪

Count: 1 trip-let 2 3 4 trip-let

THREE WAYS TO SWING IT

ACCENT ON RHYTHM: *Swing Eighth Notes*

THE BATTLE OF JERICHO

American Spiritual

ACCENT ON CONCERT F MAJOR

CHORALE: SINE NOMINE

Ralph Vaughan Williams
(1872–1958)

F MAJOR SCALE (CONCERT F)

INTERVAL WORKOUT

SCALE STUDY

CHROMATIC SCALE

ACCENT ON RHYTHM: ♫ in 6/8 Time

THE IRISH WASHERWOMAN

LIP SLUR/FLEXIBILITY STUDY

ACCENT ON CONCERT D MINOR

CHORALE: PICARDY

17th Century French Melody

D MELODIC MINOR SCALE (CONCERT D)

INTERVAL WORKOUT

*See Fingering Chart on page 38.

SCALE STUDY

D HARMONIC MINOR SCALE (CONCERT D)

ACCENT ON RHYTHM: ♩. ♩♩ in **6/8** Time

GREENSLEEVES

English Folk Song

ACCENT ON RHYTHM: ⅞ (Sixteenth Rest)

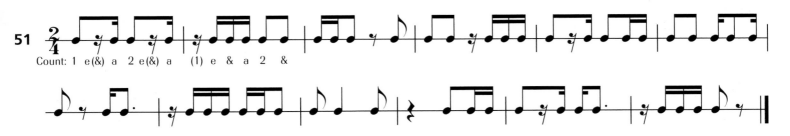

LA **C**UMPARSITA

G. Matos Rodriguez
(1897–1948)

ACCENT ON CONCERT A♭ MAJOR

CHORALE: HOW FIRM A FOUNDATION

Early American Melody

A♭ MAJOR SCALE (CONCERT A♭)

INTERVAL WORKOUT

SCALE STUDY

CHROMATIC SCALE

ACCENT ON RHYTHM: $\frac{5}{4}$ and $\frac{6}{4}$ Time

PROMENADE from "PICTURES AT AN EXHIBITION"

Modest Mussorgsky
(1839–1881)

WALTZ from "SYMPHONY NO. 6"

Peter I. Tchaikovsky
(1840–1893)

ACCENT ON CONCERT F MINOR

CHORALE: THE GOD OF ABRAHAM PRAISE

Hebrew Folk Song

61 Moderato

F MELODIC MINOR SCALE (CONCERT F)

62

INTERVAL WORKOUT

63

SCALE STUDY

64

F HARMONIC MINOR SCALE (CONCERT F)

65

ACCENT ON RHYTHM:

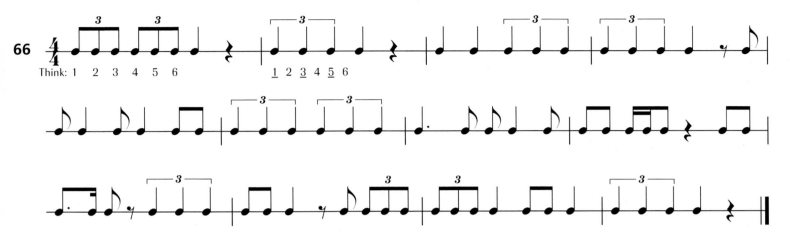

SOMETIMES I FEEL LIKE A MOTHERLESS CHILD

American Spiritual

TRIPLET TUNE

ACCENT ON CONCERT C MAJOR

CHORALE: IT IS WELL

Phillip Bliss
(1838–1876)

Moderato

ACCENT ON RHYTHM: Changing Meters — 2/4 through 6/4

SOLILOQUY

LIP SLUR/FLEXIBILITY STUDY

ACCENT ON CONCERT A MINOR

CHORALE: BASED ON A THEME BY HASSLER

Johann Sebastian Bach
(1685–1750)

A MELODIC MINOR SCALE (CONCERT A)

INTERVAL WORKOUT

SCALE STUDY

A HARMONIC MINOR SCALE (CONCERT A)

Accent on Rhythm:

ACCENT ON CONCERT Db MAJOR

CHORALE: LONDONDERRY AIR

Irish Folk Song

Andante

Db MAJOR SCALE (CONCERT Db)

*See Fingering Chart on page 38.

INTERVAL WORKOUT

SCALE STUDY

CHROMATIC SCALE

ACCENT ON RHYTHM: Changing Meters — 6/8 and 2/4

WASSAIL SONG

Traditional Carol

ACCENT ON RHYTHM: Changing Meters — 6/8 and 3/4

FIESTA MARIACHI

ACCENT ON CONCERT B♭ MINOR

CHORALE: KOMM, SÜSSER TOD

Johann Sebastian Bach
(1685–1750)

B♭ MELODIC MINOR SCALE (CONCERT B♭)

INTERVAL WORKOUT

SCALE STUDY

B♭ HARMONIC MINOR SCALE (CONCERT B♭)

ACCENT ON RHYTHM: $\frac{5}{8}$ Time

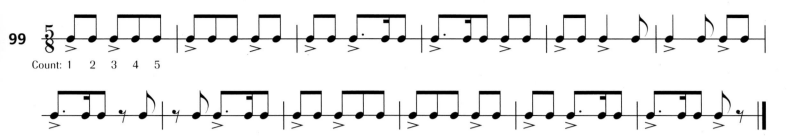

Count: 1 2 3 4 5

FUN WITH FIVE

ACCENT ON RHYTHM: Changing Meters with $\frac{3}{8}$, $\frac{5}{8}$

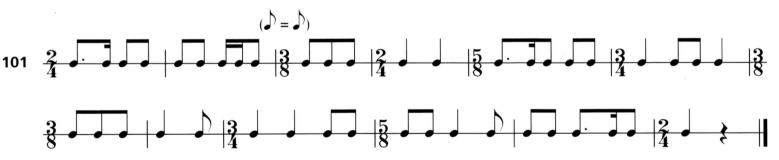

VARIATIONS ON A STAR SONG

Count: 1 2 3 4 5 6 7

ACCENT ON CONCERT G MAJOR

ACCENT ON CONCERT E MINOR

E MELODIC MINOR SCALE (CONCERT E)

INTERVAL WORKOUT

E HARMONIC MINOR SCALE (CONCERT E)

LA CINQUANTAINE

J. Gabriel-Marie
(1852–1928)

Allegretto

ACCENT ON CONCERT G♭ MAJOR

G♭ MAJOR SCALE (CONCERT G♭)

INTERVAL WORKOUT

CHROMATIC SCALE

MICHAEL, ROW THE BOAT ASHORE

American Spiritual

Andante

MARCH OF THE MEN OF HARLECH

Welsh Folk Song

Moderato

ACCENT ON CONCERT E♭ MINOR

E♭ MELODIC MINOR SCALE (CONCERT E♭)

17

INTERVAL WORKOUT

18

E♭ HARMONIC MINOR SCALE (CONCERT E♭)

19

THEME from "SWAN LAKE"

Peter I. Tchaikovsky
(1840–1893)

Andante

20

ACCENT ON CONCERT D MAJOR

D MAJOR SCALE (CONCERT D)

121

*See Fingering Chart on page 38.

INTERVAL WORKOUT

122

CHROMATIC SCALE

123

ALLELUIA

Moderato

17th Century Melody

124

SHENANDOAH

Adagio

American Folk Song

125

ACCENT ON CONCERT B MINOR

B MELODIC MINOR SCALE (CONCERT B)

126

INTERVAL WORKOUT

127

B HARMONIC MINOR SCALE (CONCERT B)

128

HATIKVAH

Israeli National Anthem

129

ACCENT ON CONCERT A MAJOR

A MAJOR SCALE (CONCERT A)

130

INTERVAL WORKOUT

131

CHROMATIC SCALE

132

BINGO

American Folk Song

133

MY BONNIE LIES OVER THE OCEAN

Traditional

134

ACCENT ON CONCERT F♯/G♭ MINOR

F♯ MELODIC MINOR SCALE (CONCERT F♯)

135

INTERVAL WORKOUT

136

F♯ HARMONIC MINOR SCALE (CONCERT F♯)

137

THEME from "SCHEHERAZADE"

Nicolai Rimsky-Korsakov
(1844–1908)

Moderato

138

ACCENT ON CONCERT C♭ MAJOR

ACCENT ON CONCERT A♭ MINOR

A♭ MELODIC MINOR SCALE (CONCERT A♭)

144

INTERVAL WORKOUT

145

A♭ HARMONIC MINOR SCALE (CONCERT A♭)

146

HAVA NAGILA

Hebrew Folk Song

Allegro

147

ACCENT ON CONCERT E MAJOR

E MAJOR SCALE (CONCERT E)

INTERVAL WORKOUT

CHROMATIC SCALE

HOME ON THE RANGE

American Folk Song

ACCENT ON CONCERT C♯/D♭ MINOR

C♯ MELODIC MINOR SCALE (CONCERT C♯)

52

INTERVAL WORKOUT

53

C♯ HARMONIC MINOR SCALE (CONCERT C♯)

54

WE THREE KINGS

Traditional Carol

Moderato

55

OBOE FINGERING CHART

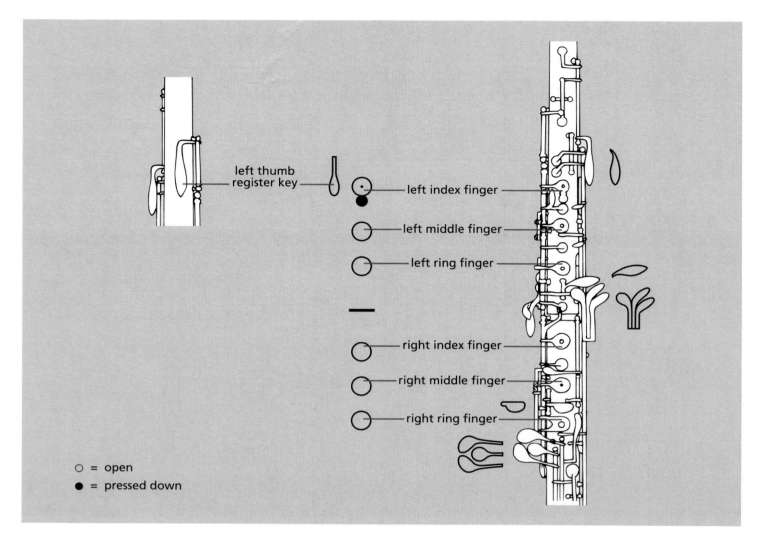

O = open
● = pressed down

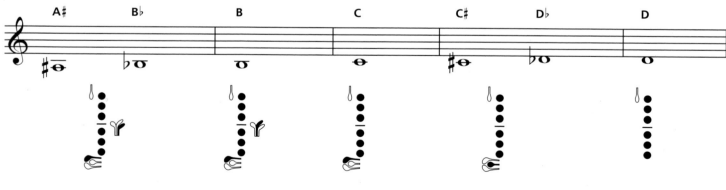

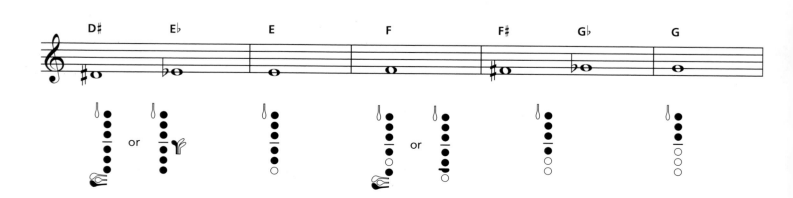

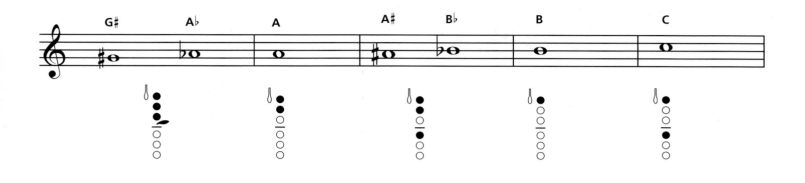

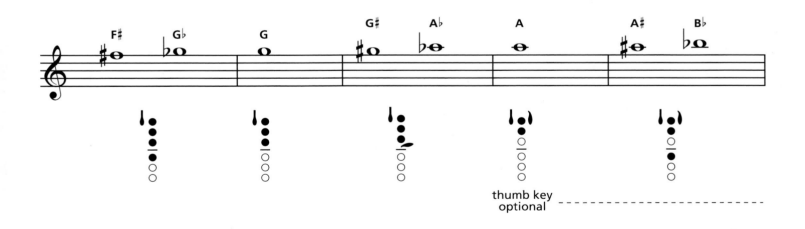

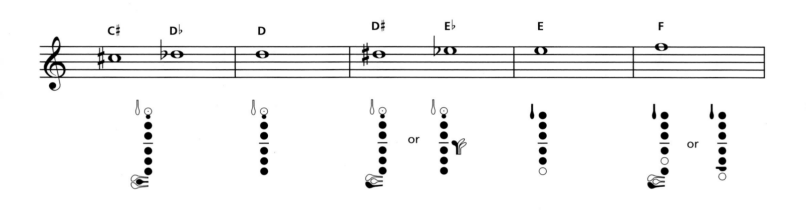

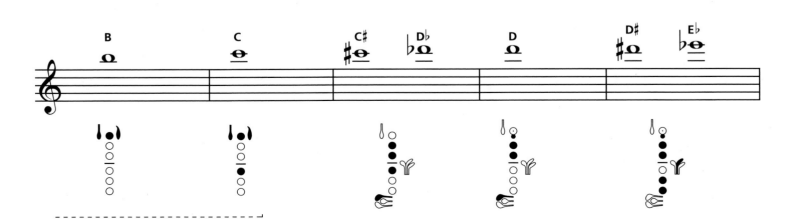

HOME PRACTICE RECORD

Week	Date	ASSIGNMENT	Mon	Tue	Wed	Thur	Fri	Sat	Sun	Total	Parent Signature
1											
2											
3											
4											
5											
6											
7											
8											
9											
10											
11											
12											
13											
14											
15											
16											
17											
18											
19											
20											
21											
22											
23											
24											
25											
26											
27											
28											
29											
30											
31											
32											
33											
34											
35											
36											